Which
Poo(dle)
for You?

A guide to selecting the right dog, designer dog
or doodle for you and your family

Paul Hill

March 2023

Table of Contents

Introduction

Owning a dog can bring a wealth of benefits to your life. Not only can dogs provide unconditional love and companionship, but they can also improve your physical and mental health by reducing stress, increasing exercise, and promoting social interaction. In addition, dogs can offer a sense of security and protection in your home. However, choosing the right dog for your lifestyle and needs is essential to ensure a happy and healthy relationship between you and your new furry friend. This book looks at many aspects of dog ownership with a particular focus on the designer "Doodle" breeds which are so popular for many reasons including their hypoallergenic coats and good nature. . In this book, we will explore the different factors to consider when choosing a dog, from breed characteristics to training and care requirements, to help you find the perfect match for you and your family

About the author

I have worked in IT for nearly forty years and have come to the world of dog ownership very late in life. My partner and our daughter decided that a dog was essential and as a result we have been blessed by the arrival of a very lovable double-doodle called Theo.

Why do people buy dogs?

There are many reasons why people buy dogs. Here are some of the most common:

Companionship: Dogs are social animals that thrive on companionship, and they make great companions for families. They provide love, affection, and a sense of security to their owners, which can be especially important for children.

Protection: Dogs are naturally protective of their owners and their homes. They have a keen sense of hearing and smell, which makes them excellent watchdogs. Many people buy dogs for protection, as they can help deter potential intruders and keep their owners safe.

Emotional Support: Dogs can also provide emotional support to their owners. They are known for their ability to reduce stress and anxiety, and they can help people feel less lonely and isolated.

Assistance: Some dogs are trained to assist people with disabilities or special needs. For example, guide dogs are trained to help people with visual impairments, while hearing dogs are trained to help people who are deaf or hard of hearing.

Working Dogs: Many dogs are bred for specific tasks, such as hunting, herding, or search and rescue. These dogs are trained to perform specific tasks and are often used for work purposes.

Exercise: Dogs need regular exercise, and many people buy dogs as a way to get more physical activity in their daily routine. Dogs need daily walks and other forms of exercise, which can help their owners stay active as well.

Teach Responsibility: Having a dog as a family pet can teach children responsibility, as they learn to feed, walk, and care for their pet. This can help children develop important life skills and a sense of empathy and compassion.

Bonding: Owning a dog as a family pet can bring family members closer together as they bond over the care and love of their pet. Dogs are known for their ability to bring joy and happiness to their owners, which can create a positive and happy environment for families.

Health Benefits: Dogs can provide many health benefits to their owners, including reduced stress and anxiety, increased physical activity, and improved heart health. Having a dog as a family pet can encourage the entire family to be more active and spend more time outdoors.

Entertainment: Dogs are playful and fun-loving, and they can provide endless entertainment and amusement for their owners. Playing with a dog can be a great way for families to relax and have fun together.

As family pets because they provide companionship, teach responsibility, and bring joy and happiness to their owners. Dogs can also provide many health benefits and act as protectors for their owners, making them valued members of many families.

Characteristics of different Breeds

Different people may look for different characteristics in dogs, depending on their lifestyle, personality, and preferences. However, here are some common characteristics that people often look for in dogs:

Temperament: Many people look for dogs with friendly, affectionate, and playful personalities. Dogs that are easy to train, obedient, and loyal are also popular choices.

Size: Some people prefer smaller dogs that are easier to handle and require less space. Others may prefer larger dogs for their protective instincts and athletic abilities.

Energy level: People often look for dogs that match their lifestyle and activity level. Active and energetic dogs are great for people who enjoy exercise and outdoor activities, while calmer dogs may be better suited for those who prefer a quieter lifestyle.

Coat type: People may look for dogs with specific coat types, such as *hypoallergenic** dogs that shed less or dogs with thick coats that are better suited for colder climates.

Purpose: Some people may look for dogs that can serve a specific purpose, such as hunting, herding, or as service dogs for people with disabilities.

Hypoallergenic Dogs

*Hypoallergenic dogs are dogs that produce fewer allergens, which can make them a great choice for people with allergies or asthma. Here are some of the benefits of hypoallergenic dogs:

Fewer allergy symptoms: People who are allergic to dogs often experience symptoms like sneezing, coughing, and itchy eyes. Hypoallergenic dogs produce less dander, saliva, and urine, which can reduce these symptoms and make it easier for people with allergies to live with dogs.

Lower risk of asthma attacks: For people with asthma, exposure to dog allergens can trigger asthma attacks. Hypoallergenic dogs produce fewer allergens, which can reduce the risk of asthma attacks and make it easier for people with asthma to live with dogs.

Less shedding: Many hypoallergenic dogs don't shed as much as other dogs, which can make them easier to manage in terms of grooming and cleaning. This can be especially beneficial for people with allergies, as shedding can spread allergens throughout the home.

Lower risk of skin irritation: Some people may experience skin irritation or rashes when they come into contact with dogs. Hypoallergenic dogs produce less dander, which can reduce the risk of skin irritation and make it easier for people with sensitive skin to live with dogs.

Easier to keep a clean home: Since hypoallergenic dogs produce fewer allergens and shed less, it can be easier to keep a clean and allergy-free home with these dogs. This can reduce the need for frequent cleaning and vacuuming, which can be a relief for busy owners.

Hypoallergenic dogs can be a great option for people with allergies or asthma who want to enjoy the companionship of a dog without suffering from symptoms. However, it's important to note that no dog is completely allergen-free, and individual reactions can vary. It's always a good idea to spend time around a hypoallergenic dog before bringing one home to make sure you don't experience any allergy symptoms.

Male or Female?

When it comes to deciding whether to get a male or female puppy, there are a few things to consider:

Temperament: In general, male dogs tend to be more dominant and aggressive than females, particularly when they have not been neutered. Female dogs are often more reserved and independent. However, each individual dog has its own personality, and it's important to meet the puppy's parents or get to know the puppy's personality before making a decision.

Size: If you have a preference for a certain size, it may be worth considering the gender of the puppy. In some breeds, males tend to be larger than females, while in others the opposite is true.

Spaying/neutering: If you are planning to spay or neuter your puppy, there are some differences to consider. Females tend to cost more to spay than males do to neuter, and females will need to have the procedure done before their first heat cycle to reduce the risk of certain health problems. Additionally, unneutered male dogs may be more likely to display certain unwanted behaviours like marking or aggression. *See also the section on Spaying/Neutering below*

The decision to get a male or female puppy should be based on your own preferences and lifestyle. Both genders can make great pets, so it's important to choose the individual puppy that you connect with and feel would be the best fit for your home.

Which Dog Breeds are known for large Males?

Many dog breeds have larger males than females, and the size difference can vary from breed to breed. Here are some dog breeds that are known for having larger males:

Great Dane: Great Danes are one of the largest dog breeds, and males can weigh up to 90 kg, while females typically weigh between 45-59 kg.

Saint Bernard: Saint Bernards are also a very large breed, and males can weigh up to 91 kg, while females typically weigh between 64-82 kg.

English Mastiff: English Mastiffs are another large breed, and males can weigh up to 113 kg, while females typically weigh between 54-91 kg.

Newfoundland: Newfoundlands are a large breed that were originally bred for working in water, and males can weigh up to 68 kg, while females typically weigh between 45-54 kg.

Irish Wolfhound: Irish Wolfhounds are one of the tallest dog breeds, and males can reach heights of up to 90 cm at the shoulder and weigh up to 68 kg, while females typically weigh between 40-55 kg.

It's important to remember that there can be variation within a breed, and individual dogs may not fit exactly within the typical weight ranges. Additionally, other factors such as genetics, nutrition, and exercise can also affect a dog's size and weight.

Which Dog Breeds are known for larger Females

While many dog breeds have larger males, there are some breeds where females tend to be larger than males. Here are some dog breeds where females are typically larger:

Saluki: Salukis are a sighthound breed that are known for their speed and grace. While males typically weigh between 20-27 kg, females can weigh up to 29 kg.

Afghan Hound: Afghan Hounds are another sighthound breed that are known for their elegant appearance. While males typically weigh between 26-34 kg, females can weigh up to 40 kg.

Basenji: Basenjis are a small breed that originated in Africa. While males typically weigh between 9-11 kg, females can weigh up to 12 kg.

Pharaoh Hound: Pharaoh Hounds are a breed that originated in Malta and are known for their athleticism and speed. While males typically weigh between 23-25 kg, females can weigh up to 28 kg.

Greyhound: Greyhounds are a sighthound breed that are often used for racing. While males typically weigh between 27-40 kg, females can weigh up to 34 kg.

There can be variation within a breed, and individual dogs may not fit exactly within the typical weight ranges. Additionally, other factors such as genetics, nutrition, and exercise can also affect a dog's size and weight.

Spaying / Neutering

Spaying and neutering are surgical procedures that remove a dog's reproductive organs to prevent them from reproducing. Spaying and neutering are common procedures recommended by veterinarians to help prevent overpopulation, reduce certain health risks, and improve behaviour in dogs. It's important to discuss the decision to spay or neuter your dog with a veterinarian and weigh the potential benefits and risks based on your individual dog's health, behaviour, and lifestyle.

Spaying, which is the procedure performed on female dogs, involves the removal of the ovaries and uterus. This prevents the female dog from going into heat and from being able to reproduce.

Neutering, which is the procedure performed on male dogs, involves the removal of the testicles. This prevents the male dog from being able to reproduce and can also reduce certain unwanted behaviours such as marking or aggression.

Both procedures are usually performed under general anaesthesia, and the dog is typically able to go home the same day as the procedure. While there may be some short-term discomfort or recovery time associated with spaying or neutering, most dogs recover quickly and are back to their normal routines within a few days.

Spaying and neutering are important considerations for any dog owner. Here are some of the factors to consider:

Health: Spaying and neutering can reduce the risk of certain health problems in dogs. For females, spaying can reduce the risk of breast cancer, uterine infections, and other reproductive issues. For males, neutering can reduce the risk of prostate problems and testicular cancer.

Behaviour: Unneutered male dogs may be more likely to display certain unwanted behaviours, such as marking territory or aggression. Female dogs may go into heat, which can lead to unwanted attention from male dogs and may cause some behavioural changes.

Overpopulation: Spaying and neutering can help reduce the number of unwanted dogs and puppies in shelters and on the streets.

Cost: The cost of spaying or neutering a dog can vary depending on factors such as the size and age of the dog, and the location of the veterinary clinic. However, it is generally less expensive than the cost of caring for an unwanted litter of puppies or treating health problems related to reproductive issues.

Timing: The best time to spay or neuter a dog can vary depending on factors such as the dog's age, breed, and health. In general, it is recommended to spay or neuter dogs between six months and one year of age, but it's important to discuss timing with a veterinarian.

The decision to spay or neuter a dog should be based on the individual dog's health, behaviour, and lifestyle, as well as the owner's preferences and values. It's important to discuss this decision with a veterinarian and weigh the potential benefits and risks of the procedure.

What types of Dogs are available?

Pedigree dogs are purebred dogs that come from a specific breed and have a documented lineage. They are often bred for specific traits and characteristics and have a predictable temperament and behaviour. Pedigree dogs are recognized by kennel clubs and can participate in dog shows.

Designer dogs, on the other hand, are a cross between two purebred dogs, often with the aim of combining desirable traits from both breeds. Designer dogs do not have a documented lineage, and their characteristics and temperament can vary widely, even within the same litter.

Designer Poodle Crossbreeds, commonly known as "doodles," (designer poodles) are a popular type of designer dog that are often touted as great pets for families. There is more information on these below.

When considering whether to buy a pedigree or designer dog, it is essential to research the breeds thoroughly and make sure you understand the potential health issues and personality traits of each breed. You should also consider the ethical implications of breeding and purchasing designer dogs, as there is some controversy surrounding the practice.

Pedigree Dogs

There are many different types of pedigree dogs, with each breed having its unique characteristics, history, and traits. Here are some examples of common pedigree dog breeds:

Labrador Retriever

Labrador Retrievers are known for their friendly and outgoing personalities, as well as their intelligence and trainability. Here are some common traits of the Labrador Retriever breed:

Affectionate: Labrador Retrievers are known for their love of people and their affectionate nature. They enjoy being around their family and are often eager to cuddle and give kisses.

Energetic: Labrador Retrievers are high-energy dogs that love to play and exercise. They require daily exercise to keep them healthy and happy.

Intelligent: Labrador Retrievers are intelligent dogs that are easy to train. They are quick learners and are often used as service dogs, hunting dogs, and in other working roles.

Friendly: Labrador Retrievers are known for their friendly personalities and their love of other dogs and people. They are generally good with children and other pets.

Loyal: Labrador Retrievers are loyal dogs that form strong bonds with their families. They are often protective of their loved ones and will go to great lengths to keep them safe.

Good with water: Labrador Retrievers are often used as water dogs because they have a natural love of water and are excellent swimmers.

Food motivated: Labrador Retrievers love to eat and can be prone to *overeating* if not given proper portion control and exercise.

Labrador Retrievers are loyal, friendly, and intelligent dogs that make great companions for active families. They do require regular exercise and training to keep them happy and healthy.

German Shepherd

German Shepherds are a breed of dog that were originally developed for herding sheep but have since become popular as working dogs, family pets, and in law enforcement and military roles. Here are some common traits of the German Shepherd breed:

Intelligent: German Shepherds are highly intelligent and are often used as service dogs, search and rescue dogs, and in other working roles. They are quick learners and can be easily trained for a variety of tasks.

Protective: German Shepherds are known for their loyalty and protective instincts. They are often used as guard dogs and can be fiercely protective of their families and homes.

Energetic: German Shepherds are active dogs that require regular exercise to keep them healthy and happy. They enjoy playing and going for walks or runs with their owners.

Courageous: German Shepherds are brave dogs that are not easily intimidated. They are often used in law enforcement and military roles because of their courage and determination.

Good with children: German Shepherds can be great with children *if socialised properly*. They are often patient and gentle with kids and can make good family pets.

High prey drive: German Shepherds have a strong prey drive and may be prone to chasing small animals such as cats or squirrels.

Shedding: German Shepherds have a double coat that sheds heavily, particularly during shedding season. They require regular grooming to keep their coat healthy and clean.

German Shepherds are intelligent, loyal, and protective dogs that make great working dogs, family pets, and companions. They do require regular exercise and training, as well as socialization, to keep them healthy and happy.

Golden Retriever

Golden Retrievers are a breed of dog that were originally developed for hunting purposes, but have since become popular as family pets and therapy dogs. Here are some common traits of the Golden Retriever breed:

Friendly: Golden Retrievers are known for their friendly and outgoing personalities. They are often described as "people pleasers" and are eager to please their owners.

Intelligent: Golden Retrievers are intelligent dogs that are easy to train. They are often used as service dogs and in other working roles.

Affectionate: Golden Retrievers are known for their love of people and their affectionate nature. They enjoy being around their family and are often eager to cuddle and give kisses.

Energetic: Golden Retrievers are high-energy dogs that love to play and exercise. They require daily exercise to keep them healthy and happy.

Good with children: Golden Retrievers are often great with children and can make good family pets. They are generally patient and gentle with kids.

Retrieving instinct: Golden Retrievers were originally bred for hunting and have a strong instinct to retrieve. They enjoy playing fetch and can be trained to retrieve objects such as balls or frisbees.

Shedding: Golden Retrievers have a dense, water-repellent coat that sheds heavily, particularly during shedding season. They require regular grooming to keep their coat healthy and clean.

Golden Retrievers are friendly, intelligent, and affectionate dogs that make great family pets and therapy dogs. They do require regular exercise and grooming to keep them healthy and happy.

Bulldog

Bulldogs are a breed of dog that are known for their distinctive appearance and unique personality. Here are some common traits of the Bulldog breed:

Stubborn: Bulldogs are known for their stubbornness and can be difficult to train. They require consistent and patient training to learn new commands and behaviours.

Affectionate: Bulldogs are known for their affectionate and loyal personalities. They enjoy spending time with their families and are often described as "lap dogs."

Protective: Bulldogs are often protective of their families and can be wary of strangers. They make good watchdogs and can be trained to protect their home and family.

Low-energy: Bulldogs are generally low-energy dogs that enjoy lounging around the house. They do require daily exercise, but they do not need as much activity as some other breeds.

Health issues: Bulldogs are prone to a variety of health issues, including respiratory problems, skin allergies, and joint problems. It is important to take proper care of their health and work closely with a veterinarian to manage any health concerns.

Facial wrinkles: Bulldogs have facial wrinkles that require regular cleaning to prevent infection or irritation. They also require regular grooming to maintain their coat and overall health.

Friendly: Despite their sometimes gruff appearance, Bulldogs are generally friendly dogs that enjoy being around people. They can be good with children and make good family pets.

Bulldogs are affectionate, protective, and low-energy dogs that require careful attention to their health and hygiene needs. They make good companions for families or individuals who are looking for a loyal and loving pet.

Beagle

Beagles are a breed of dog that were originally developed for hunting purposes. Here are some common traits of the Beagle breed:

Playful: Beagles are known for their playful and energetic personalities. They enjoy playing with their owners and other dogs.

Friendly: Beagles are generally friendly dogs that get along well with people and other dogs. They can make good family pets.

Inquisitive: Beagles have a strong sense of smell and are naturally curious dogs. They can be easily distracted by interesting scents, which can make training a challenge.

Vocal: Beagles are known for their distinctive howling and barking. They are often used as hunting dogs because of their vocalisations.

Good with children: Beagles are often good with children and can make good family pets. They are generally patient and gentle with kids.

High energy: Beagles are high-energy dogs that require daily exercise to keep them healthy and happy. They enjoy going for walks and playing outside.

Strong prey drive: Beagles were originally bred for hunting small game such as rabbits, and they have a strong prey drive. They may be prone to chasing small animals such as cats or squirrels.

Beagles are friendly, playful, and curious dogs that make good companions for active families or individuals.

Poodle

Although I'm mainly discussing designer dogs in this book and focussing on designer Poodle crossbreeds ("Doodles"), I'm going to start with a purebred poodle for comparison. There are many benefits to owning a poodle! Here are some of the most common ones:

Low-shedding: Poodles have hair instead of fur, which means they shed very little. This makes them a great choice for people with allergies or those who don't want to deal with a lot of pet hair.

Intelligent: Poodles are one of the most intelligent dog breeds and are known for their trainability. They are quick learners and can be easily taught commands and tricks.

Good with children: Poodles are generally good with children and make great family pets. They are patient, gentle, and playful, making them a great companion for kids.

Hypoallergenic: While no dog is completely hypoallergenic, poodles are considered one of the best breeds for people with allergies. Because they don't shed much, they produce less dander, which is the main allergen.

Athletic: Poodles are very active dogs and love to play and exercise. They are great companions for people who enjoy outdoor activities like hiking, running, or swimming.

Versatile: Poodles come in three sizes (toy, miniature, and standard) and can be bred with other breeds to create "designer dogs" like the Labradoodle and the Cockapoo. This means that there is a poodle for almost every lifestyle and living situation.

Good health: Poodles are generally a healthy breed and have a long lifespan. They are prone to some health issues like hip dysplasia and eye problems, but with proper care and regular veterinary check-ups, they can live happy, healthy lives.

Poodles make great pets for many different people. They are intelligent, affectionate, athletic, and hypoallergenic, which makes them a great choice for families, individuals, and people with allergies.

Rottweiler

Rottweilers are large, muscular dogs with a distinctive black and tan coat. Here are some common traits of the breed:

Loyalty: Rottweilers are known for their loyalty and devotion to their owners.

Intelligence: Rottweilers are intelligent dogs that are quick to learn and eager to please.

Protective: Rottweilers have a strong protective instinct and can be wary of strangers.

Courageous: Rottweilers are brave dogs that are not easily intimidated.

Affectionate: Despite their tough exterior, Rottweilers can be very affectionate and loving towards their family.

Active: Rottweilers are active dogs that require regular exercise to stay healthy and happy.

Confident: Rottweilers have a confident and self-assured demeanour.

Dominant: Rottweilers can be dominant dogs and require a strong, consistent owner who can provide them with proper training and socialisation.

It's important to note that while these traits are common among Rottweilers, individual dogs can vary in temperament and behaviour based on their genetics, environment, and upbringing. Proper socialization and training are key to raising a well-behaved and happy Rottweiler.

Yorkshire Terrier

Yorkshire Terriers, also known as Yorkies, are small, energetic dogs with a distinct personality. Here are some common traits of the breed:

Loyal: Yorkies are known for their strong loyalty to their owners and often form a close bond with them.

Playful: Yorkies have a playful and energetic personality and love to play with toys and go on walks.

Alert: Yorkies are naturally alert dogs and make good watchdogs due to their tendency to bark at unfamiliar sounds or people.

Confident: Yorkies have a confident and bold personality, despite their small size.

Intelligent: Yorkies are intelligent dogs and are generally quick to learn new tricks and commands.

Independent: Yorkies can be independent and may prefer to spend time alone at times.

Protective: Despite their small size, Yorkies can be protective of their owners and may become aggressive towards strangers or other dogs.

Stubborn: Yorkies can be stubborn and may require patience and persistence during training.

It's important to note that while these traits are common among Yorkies, individual dogs can vary in temperament and behaviour based on their genetics, environment, and upbringing. Proper socialisation and training are key to raising a well-behaved and happy Yorkshire Terrier.

Boxer

Boxers are medium to large-sized dogs with a distinctive muscular build and a short, smooth coat. Here are some common traits of the breed:

Energetic: Boxers are high-energy dogs and require regular exercise and playtime to stay healthy and happy.

Playful: Boxers have a playful and silly personality and love to play with toys and their owners.

Loyal: Boxers are known for their loyalty and devotion to their owners and often form a close bond with them.

Intelligent: Boxers are intelligent dogs that are quick to learn and eager to please their owners.

Protective: Boxers have a strong protective instinct and can be wary of strangers, making them good watchdogs.

Affectionate: Boxers are affectionate dogs and often enjoy cuddling with their owners.

Confident: Boxers have a confident and self-assured demeanour and can be quite stubborn at times.

Active: Boxers are an active breed and require plenty of physical activity and mental stimulation.

It's important to note that while these traits are common among Boxers, individual dogs can vary in temperament and behaviour based on their genetics, environment, and upbringing. Proper socialization and training are key to raising a well-behaved and happy Boxer

Dalmatian

Dalmatians are a medium-sized breed with a distinctive white coat and black or liver spots. Here are some common traits of the breed:

Energetic: Dalmatians are high-energy dogs and require plenty of exercise and playtime to stay healthy and happy.

Playful: Dalmatians have a playful and silly personality and enjoy playing games and running around with their owners.

Intelligent: Dalmatians are intelligent dogs that are quick to learn and enjoy learning new tricks and commands.

Affectionate: Dalmatians are affectionate dogs and often enjoy spending time with their owners and cuddling.

Loyal: Dalmatians are known for their loyalty and devotion to their owners and can be protective of them.

Independent: Dalmatians can be independent dogs and may prefer to have some alone time.

Stubborn: Dalmatians can be stubborn and may require patience and persistence during training.

Sensitive: Dalmatians are sensitive dogs and may not respond well to harsh training methods or a harsh tone of voice.

It's important to note that while these traits are common among Dalmatians, individual dogs can vary in temperament and behaviour based on their genetics, environment, and upbringing. Proper socialisation and training are key to raising a well-behaved and happy Dalmatian.

Siberian Husky

Siberian Huskies are a medium-sized breed known for their thick fur and distinctive markings. Here are some common traits of the breed:

Energetic: Huskies are high-energy dogs and require plenty of exercise and playtime to stay healthy and happy.

Playful: Huskies have a playful and curious personality and enjoy playing games and exploring their surroundings.

Intelligent: Huskies are intelligent dogs and are quick learners. They also have a strong independent streak.

Affectionate: Huskies are affectionate dogs and enjoy spending time with their owners.

Loyal: Huskies are loyal dogs and can form a strong bond with their owners.

Friendly: Huskies are generally friendly dogs and enjoy meeting new people and other dogs.

Vocal: Huskies are a vocal breed and often communicate with their owners through barks, howls, and whines.

Independent: Huskies can be independent and may not always follow commands if they are not motivated.

It's important to note that while these traits are common among Huskies, individual dogs can vary in temperament and behaviour based on their genetics, environment, and upbringing. Proper socialisation and training are key to raising a well-behaved and happy Siberian Husky.

Chihuahua

Chihuahuas are a small breed of dog known for their petite size and big personalities. Here are some common traits of the breed:

Lively: Chihuahuas are lively and energetic dogs that require regular exercise and playtime to stay healthy and happy.

Alert: Chihuahuas are naturally alert dogs and make good watchdogs due to their tendency to bark at unfamiliar sounds or people.

Affectionate: Chihuahuas are affectionate dogs that often form close bonds with their owners and enjoy cuddling and snuggling.

Intelligent: Chihuahuas are intelligent dogs that are quick to learn and can be trained easily.

Bold: Despite their small size, Chihuahuas have a bold and confident personality and can be quite fearless.

Independent: Chihuahuas can be independent and may prefer to spend time alone at times.

Protective: Chihuahuas have a strong protective instinct and can be fiercely loyal to their owners.

Stubborn: Chihuahuas can be stubborn and may require patience and persistence during training.

While these traits are common among Chihuahuas, individual dogs can vary in temperament and behaviour based on their genetics, environment, and upbringing. Proper socialization and training are key to raising a well-behaved and happy Chihuahua.

Great Dane

Great Danes are a large breed of dogs that are known for their elegance and strength. Here are some common traits of Great Danes:

Size: Great Danes are one of the largest breeds of dogs, standing up to 80 cm tall at the shoulder and weighing up to 80 kg or even more.

Temperament: Great Danes are known for their gentle, friendly, and sociable nature. They are good with children and make great family pets.

Appearance: Great Danes have a muscular build with a sleek, shiny coat that can come in a variety of colours, including black, blue, fawn, brindle, and harlequin.

Intelligence: Great Danes are intelligent and trainable dogs. They are quick learners and respond well to positive reinforcement training methods.

Exercise: Great Danes need regular exercise to keep them healthy and happy. They require daily walks and playtime in a secure, fenced-in yard.

Health: Great Danes are prone to certain health problems, such as hip dysplasia, bloat, and heart disease. Regular vet check-ups are important to maintain their overall health.

Lifespan: Great Danes have a shorter lifespan compared to smaller breeds, typically living between 6 to 8 years.

Doberman Pinscher

Doberman Pinschers are a breed of dog that are known for their intelligence, loyalty, and protective nature. Here are some common traits of Doberman Pinschers:

Size: Doberman Pinschers are medium to large-sized dogs, standing up to 72 cm tall at the shoulder and weighing up to 45 kg.

Temperament: Doberman Pinschers are known for their loyalty and protective nature. They are highly intelligent, and when trained properly, they are obedient and easy to manage.

Appearance: Doberman Pinschers have a sleek, muscular build with a short, shiny coat that can come in a variety of colours, including black, blue, fawn, and red.

Intelligence: Doberman Pinschers are highly intelligent dogs and are known for their trainability. They excel in obedience training, agility, and other dog sports.

Exercise: Doberman Pinschers require daily exercise to keep them healthy and happy. They need regular walks and playtime in a secure, fenced-in yard.

Health: Doberman Pinschers are prone to certain health problems, such as hip dysplasia, von Willebrand's disease, and dilated cardiomyopathy. Regular vet check-ups are important to maintain their overall health.

Lifespan: Doberman Pinschers have a lifespan of about 10 to 13 years.

Shih Tzu

Shih Tzus are a small breed of dog that are known for their affectionate, playful, and charming personalities. Here are some common traits of Shih Tzus:

Size: Shih Tzus are a small breed of dog, standing up to 28 cm tall at the shoulder and weighing up to 7.5 kg.

Temperament: Shih Tzus are known for their affectionate, playful, and charming personalities. They are friendly and outgoing, and they tend to get along well with other animals and children.

Appearance: Shih Tzus have a long, silky coat that comes in a variety of colours, including black, white, brown, and gold. They have a round head and a short snout, with large, expressive eyes.

Intelligence: Shih Tzus are intelligent dogs, but they can be stubborn at times. They are relatively easy to train, but they require consistent and patient training methods.

Exercise: Shih Tzus are small dogs that don't require a lot of exercise. They enjoy short walks and indoor playtime with their owners.

Health: Shih Tzus are prone to certain health problems, such as dental issues, eye problems, and breathing difficulties. Regular vet check-ups are important to maintain their overall health.

Lifespan: Shih Tzus have a lifespan of about 10 to 16 years.

Terriers

There are many different types of terriers, each with their own distinct traits and characteristics. Here are some of the most popular terrier breeds:

Airedale Terrier: Airedales are large terriers that were originally bred for hunting. They are intelligent, energetic, and loyal dogs.

American Staffordshire Terrier: Also known as Amstaffs, these dogs are muscular and strong. They are known for their courage and loyalty, but can also be stubborn.

Border Terrier: Border Terriers are small, scrappy dogs that were originally bred for hunting vermin. They are intelligent, active, and friendly.

Boston Terrier: Boston Terriers are small, compact dogs that are known for their affectionate and playful personalities. They are often referred to as "the American Gentleman" because of their tuxedo-like coat.

Bull Terrier: Bull Terriers are muscular and athletic dogs that were originally bred for bullbaiting. They are known for their loyalty and affectionate personalities.

Cairn Terrier: Cairn Terriers are small, scrappy dogs that were originally bred for hunting. They are known for their courage and determination, and are often described as "big dogs in small bodies."

Jack Russell Terrier: Jack Russells are small, energetic dogs that were originally bred for hunting. They are intelligent, lively, and independent.

Scottish Terrier: Also known as Scotties, these dogs are small, sturdy, and independent. They are known for their loyalty and courage.

West Highland White Terrier: Also known as Westies, these dogs are small, energetic, and friendly. They are known for their white, fluffy coat and lively personalities.

These are just a few of the many different types of terriers that are out there. Each breed has its own unique set of characteristics and traits that make them special and beloved by their owners.

Designer Dogs / Crossbreeds

Designer dogs are a relatively new type of dog that are created by crossbreeding two different purebred dogs. These dogs are sometimes referred to as "hybrid dogs" or "designer breeds." The goal of breeding designer dogs is to create a dog with the best characteristics of both breeds, such as a hypoallergenic coat, intelligence, or a specific temperament.

Some popular examples of designer dogs include:

- Goldendoodle (Golden Retriever + Poodle)
- Labradoodle (Labrador Retriever + Poodle)
- Cockapoo (Cocker Spaniel + Poodle)
- Pomsky (Pomeranian + Siberian Husky)
- Cavachon (Cavalier King Charles Spaniel + Bichon Frise)
- Schnoodle (Schnauzer + Poodle)
- Yorkipoo (Yorkshire Terrier + Poodle)
- Maltipoo (Maltese + Poodle)

It's important to note that designer dogs are not recognized as a breed by major kennel clubs, as they are not considered to be a purebred. As with any breed or type of dog, it's essential to research and understand the characteristics and needs of both parent breeds before deciding on a designer dog.

Here are some characteristics and benefits of designer dogs:

Hypoallergenic coats - Some designer dogs, such as the Poodle mix breeds, are known for their hypoallergenic coats. This can be beneficial for individuals who have allergies to dogs or who want a dog that sheds less.

Unique appearance - Designer dogs can have a unique and distinctive appearance that sets them apart from other breeds. This can be a desirable trait for individuals who want a dog that looks different from traditional purebred breeds.

Potential health benefits - Crossbreeding can sometimes reduce the likelihood of genetic health issues that are common in purebred dogs. For example, Labradoodles are less prone to hip dysplasia than their purebred Labrador Retriever counterparts.

Personality traits - Designer dogs can inherit positive personality traits from both parent breeds. For example, a Goldendoodle may inherit the friendly and social nature of a Golden Retriever and the intelligence and trainability of a Poodle.

Size - Designer dogs can come in a range of sizes, from small to large. This can be beneficial for individuals who have specific size requirements or limitations in their living space.

Energy level - Designer dogs can have a variety of energy levels, from high-energy to low-energy. This can be beneficial for individuals who want a dog that matches their lifestyle and activity level.

Trainability - Many designer dogs are highly intelligent and trainable, which can make them easier to train than some purebred dogs. This can be beneficial for individuals who want a dog that is easy to train and eager to please.

It's important to note that not all designer dogs will inherit these characteristics, and there is always some variability in temperament and physical traits within any breed or crossbreed. Additionally, it's essential to research and understand the potential health issues that can arise from crossbreeding and to work with a reputable breeder who prioritizes the health and well-being of their dogs.

Poodle Mixes (Doodles)

Designer Poodle Crossbreeds, commonly known as "doodles," (designer poodles) are a popular type of designer dog that are often touted as great pets for families. There are several reasons why this is the case:

Low-shedding: Poodles have hair rather than fur, which means they shed less than many other dog breeds. When poodles are crossed with other breeds, the resulting doodles often inherit this low-shedding trait, making them a good choice for families with allergies or those who don't want to deal with excessive shedding. It's important to note that while Poodle mixes are often touted as hypoallergenic, not all Poodle mixes are hypoallergenic and individual dogs can vary in their coat type and shedding tendencies.

Intelligent: Poodles are highly intelligent dogs, and their doodle offspring often inherit this trait. This makes them easier to train and teach commands, which can make them a great fit for families with children.

Affectionate: Poodles and their mixes are known for their affectionate personalities. They enjoy spending time with their families and are often very loyal to their owners. This can make them a great companion for children and adults alike.

Versatile: Doodles come in a variety of sizes and can be bred with many different dog breeds, which means there is a doodle out there for almost any family. Whether you want a small lap dog or a larger breed for outdoor activities, there is likely a doodle that will fit your needs.

Health: Although no dog breed is completely immune to health problems, poodles and their mixes are generally considered to be healthy dogs. This means they are less likely to develop health issues that can be costly to treat, which can be a relief for families on a budget.

Poodle mixes can make great pets for families due to their low-shedding, intelligence, affectionate nature, versatility, and good health. There are many different types of poodle mix and we will examine the benefits of each individually below.

Labradoodle (Labrador Retriever + Poodle)

- Standard Labradoodles: 22-29 kg
- Medium Labradoodles: 13-20 kg
- Miniature Labradoodles: 7-11 kg

Labradoodles are a hybrid dog breed that is a cross between a Labrador Retriever and a Standard Poodle or a Miniature Poodle. Since Labradoodles are a mixed breed, here are some common characteristics:

Low shedding: Labradoodles are often bred for their low-shedding coat, making them a good choice for people with allergies or who don't want to deal with excessive shedding.

Intelligent: Both Labrador Retrievers and Poodles are intelligent breeds, so Labradoodles tend to be smart and trainable.

Affectionate: Labradoodles are known for their affectionate and friendly personalities. They tend to be social dogs that enjoy spending time with their owners and are often good with children.

Active: Labradoodles have a lot of energy and need regular exercise and playtime. They do well in active households or with owners who can provide them with plenty of exercise.

Versatile: Labradoodles come in different sizes, depending on the size of the Poodle parent, and can be bred with other breeds to create different designer dogs. This means that there is a Labradoodle out there for almost any lifestyle.

Coat variety: Labradoodles can have a range of coat types, including wavy, curly, or straight. Some have a smooth, short coat like a Labrador Retriever, while others have a longer, shaggier coat like a Poodle.

Health: While mixed breed dogs can be prone to some of the health issues that their parent breeds are known for, Labradoodles tend to be a healthy breed overall.

Labradoodles tend to be intelligent, affectionate, and active dogs that do well in a variety of households.

Goldendoodle (Golden Retriever + Poodle)

- Standard Goldendoodles: 20-40 kg
- Medium Goldendoodles: 13-20 kg
- Miniature Goldendoodles: 7-13 kg

Goldendoodles are a hybrid dog breed that is a cross between a Golden Retriever and a Standard Poodle or a Miniature Poodle. Like Labradoodles, Goldendoodles are a mixed breed, so their traits can vary depending on the individual dog. Here are some common characteristics:

Low shedding: Goldendoodles are often bred for their low-shedding coat, making them a good choice for people with allergies or who don't want to deal with excessive shedding.

Intelligent: Both Golden Retrievers and Poodles are intelligent breeds, so Goldendoodles tend to be smart and trainable.

Affectionate: Goldendoodles are known for their affectionate and friendly personalities. They tend to be social dogs that enjoy spending time with their owners and are often good with children.

Active: Goldendoodles have a lot of energy and need regular exercise and playtime. They do well in active households or with owners who can provide them with plenty of exercise.

Versatile: Goldendoodles come in different sizes, depending on the size of the Poodle parent, and can be bred with other breeds to create different designer dogs. This means that there is a Goldendoodle out there for almost any lifestyle.

Coat variety: Goldendoodles can have a range of coat types, including wavy, curly, or straight. Some have a smooth, short coat like a Golden Retriever, while others have a longer, shaggier coat like a Poodle.

Health: While mixed breed dogs can be prone to some of the health issues that their parent breeds are known for, Goldendoodles tend to be a healthy breed overall.

Goldendoodles tend to be intelligent, affectionate, and active dogs that do well in a variety of households.

Cockapoo – (Cocker Spaniel + Poodle)

Cockapoos are a popular breed of mixed dogs that are a cross between a Cocker Spaniel and a Poodle. Here are some common traits of Cockapoos:

Size: Cockapoos come in different sizes depending on their parents. They can be small or medium-sized dogs, ranging from 25 to 38 cm in height and weighing between 5 to 11 kg.

Temperament: Cockapoos are known for their friendly and sociable personalities. They are affectionate dogs that get along well with people, other dogs, and pets.

Appearance: Cockapoos have a soft, curly coat that can come in a variety of colours, including black, white, cream, brown, and red. Their coat is usually low-shedding, which makes them a good choice for people with allergies.

Intelligence: Cockapoos are intelligent and easy to train dogs. They have a strong desire to please their owners and respond well to positive reinforcement training methods.

Exercise: Cockapoos require daily exercise to stay healthy and happy. They enjoy walks, playtime in the yard, and indoor play sessions with their owners.

Health: Cockapoos are generally healthy dogs, but they may be prone to some health problems inherited from their parent breeds, such as ear infections, skin allergies, and hip dysplasia. Regular vet check-ups and proper grooming can help prevent health issues.

Lifespan: Cockapoos have a lifespan of about 12 to 15 years.

Schnoodle – (Schnauzer + Poodle)

Schnoodles are a mixed breed of dog that are a cross between a Schnauzer and a Poodle. Here are some common traits of Schnoodles:

Size: Schnoodles come in different sizes depending on their parents. They can be small or medium-sized dogs, ranging from 25 to 46 cm in height and weighing between 3.6 to 16 kg.

Temperament: Schnoodles are known for their friendly and sociable personalities. They are affectionate dogs that get along well with people, other dogs, and pets.

Appearance: Schnoodles have a soft, curly coat that can come in a variety of colours, including black, white, cream, brown, and grey. Their coat is usually low-shedding, which makes them a good choice for people with allergies.

Intelligence: Schnoodles are intelligent and easy to train dogs. They have a strong desire to please their owners and respond well to positive reinforcement training methods.

Exercise: Schnoodles require daily exercise to stay healthy and happy. They enjoy walks, playtime in the yard, and indoor play sessions with their owners.

Health: Schnoodles are generally healthy dogs, but they may be prone to some health problems inherited from their parent breeds, such as hip dysplasia, eye problems, and skin allergies. Regular vet check-ups and proper grooming can help prevent health issues.

Lifespan: Schnoodles have a lifespan of about 10 to 15 years.

Yorkipoo – (Yorkshire Terrier + Poodle)

Yorkipoos are a mixed breed of dog that are a cross between a Yorkshire Terrier and a Poodle. Here are some common traits of Yorkipoos:

Size: Yorkipoos are small dogs, typically weighing between 2.2 to 6.8 kg and standing 15 to 23 cm tall at the shoulder.

Temperament: Yorkipoos are known for their friendly and affectionate personalities. They are social dogs that enjoy spending time with their owners and other people.

Appearance: Yorkipoos have a curly or wavy coat that can come in a variety of colours, including black, white, brown, and grey. Their coat is usually low-shedding, which makes them a good choice for people with allergies.

Intelligence: Yorkipoos are intelligent and trainable dogs. They are quick learners and respond well to positive reinforcement training methods.

Exercise: Yorkipoos require daily exercise to stay healthy and happy. They enjoy short walks, indoor play sessions, and playing in the yard.

Health: Yorkipoos are generally healthy dogs, but they may be prone to some health problems inherited from their parent breeds, such as dental problems, eye problems, and skin allergies. Regular vet check-ups and proper grooming can help prevent health issues.

Lifespan: Yorkipoos have a lifespan of about 10 to 15 years.

Bernedoodle – (Bernese Mountain Dog + Poodle)

- Standard Bernedoodle: 32-40 kg
- Medium Bernedoodle: 18-32 kg
- Miniature Bernedoodle: 11-22 kg

Bernedoodles are a mixed breed of dog that are a cross between a Bernese Mountain Dog and a Poodle. Here are some common traits of Bernedoodles:

Size: Bernedoodles come in different sizes depending on their parents. They can be small, medium or large dogs, ranging from 45 to 75 cm in height and weighing between 18 to 40 kg.

Temperament: Bernedoodles are known for their friendly and affectionate personalities. They are social dogs that enjoy spending time with their owners and other people. They are also known for being great with children and other pets.

Appearance: Bernedoodles have a wavy or curly coat that can come in a variety of colours, including black, white, brown, and grey. Their coat is usually low-shedding, which makes them a good choice for people with allergies.

Intelligence: Bernedoodles are intelligent and trainable dogs. They are quick learners and respond well to positive reinforcement training methods.

Exercise: Bernedoodles require daily exercise to stay healthy and happy. They enjoy walks, playtime in the yard, and indoor play sessions with their owners.

Health: Bernedoodles are generally healthy dogs, but they may be prone to some health problems inherited from their parent breeds, such as hip dysplasia, eye problems, and skin allergies. Regular vet check-ups and proper grooming can help prevent health issues.

Lifespan: Bernedoodles have a lifespan of about 12 to 15 years.

Whoodle – (Wheaten Terrier + Poodle)

A Whoodle is a hybrid dog breed that results from crossing a Poodle with a Soft Coated Wheaten Terrier. The traits of a Whoodle can vary depending on the parent breeds' characteristics and the specific dog's genetic makeup, but here are some general traits commonly seen in Whoodles:

Size: Whoodles are usually medium-sized dogs, ranging in weight from 20 to 45 pounds and standing around 12 to 20 inches tall at the shoulder.

Coat: Whoodles have a soft, wavy, or curly coat that is usually hypoallergenic and low-shedding, making them a good choice for people with allergies.

Colour: Whoodles can come in a variety of colours, including black, white, cream, apricot, and red.

Temperament: Whoodles are known for their friendly, outgoing personalities and their ability to get along well with children and other pets. They are also intelligent and eager to please, which makes them easy to train.

Exercise needs: Whoodles have moderate exercise needs and require daily walks and playtime to keep them physically and mentally stimulated.

Health: Like all dog breeds, Whoodles can be prone to certain health issues, such as hip dysplasia and eye problems. It's essential to buy a Whoodle puppy from a reputable breeder who tests their breeding dogs for genetic health conditions.

Overall, Whoodles make excellent family pets that are affectionate, playful, and adaptable to different living environments.

Aussiedoodle - Australian Shepherd + Poodle

An Aussiedoodle is a hybrid dog breed that results from crossing a Poodle with an Australian Shepherd. The traits of an Aussiedoodle can vary depending on the parent breeds' characteristics and the specific dog's genetic makeup, but here are some general traits commonly seen in Aussiedoodles:

Size: Aussiedoodles can range in size from small to medium-sized dogs, depending on the size of the Poodle parent. They typically weigh between 25 to 70 pounds and stand around 12 to 23 inches tall at the shoulder.

Coat: Aussiedoodles have a soft, curly or wavy coat that can be long or medium length. They may be hypoallergenic and low-shedding, making them a good choice for people with allergies.

Colour: Aussiedoodles can come in a variety of colours, including black, white, cream, blue, merle, and red.

Temperament: Aussiedoodles are known for their friendly, loyal, and intelligent personalities. They are highly trainable and make excellent family pets, as they are good with children and other pets.

Exercise needs: Aussiedoodle have high exercise needs and require daily physical activity and mental stimulation to prevent boredom and destructive behaviour.

Health: Like all dog breeds, Aussiedoodles can be prone to certain health issues, such as hip dysplasia and eye problems. It's essential to buy an Aussiedoodle puppy from a reputable breeder who tests their breeding dogs for genetic health conditions.

Aussiedoodles are a popular breed that combines the intelligence and trainability of the Poodle with the loyal and affectionate nature of the Australian Shepherd. They make excellent family pets for active households who can provide them with the exercise and attention they need.

Bichonpoo -/ Poochon (Bichon Frise + Poodle)

A Bichonpoo, also known as a Bichpoo or Poochon, is a hybrid dog breed that results from crossing a Poodle with a Bichon Frise. The traits of a Bichonpoo can vary depending on the parent breeds' characteristics and the specific dog's genetic makeup, but here are some general traits commonly seen in Bichonpoos:

Size: Bichonpoos are small to medium-sized dogs, typically weighing between 7kg to 8.5kg and standing around 22 to 28cm tall at the shoulder.

Coat: Bichonpoos have a soft, curly, or wavy coat that can be hypoallergenic and low-shedding, making them a good choice for people with allergies.

Colour: Bichonpoos can come in a variety of colours, including white, cream, apricot, and black.

Temperament: Bichonpoos are known for their friendly, affectionate, and playful personalities. They are good with children and other pets and make excellent family pets.

Exercise needs: Bichonpoos have moderate exercise needs and require daily walks and playtime to keep them physically and mentally stimulated.

Health: Like all dog breeds, Bichonpoos can be prone to certain health issues, such as hip dysplasia, ear infections, and dental problems. It's essential to buy a Bichonpoo puppy from a reputable breeder who tests their breeding dogs for genetic health conditions.

Bichonpoos are a popular breed that combines the intelligence and trainability of the Poodle with the affectionate and playful nature of the Bichon Frise. They make excellent family pets for people who are looking for a small, hypoallergenic dog that is easy to train and loves to play.

Cavapoo – (Cavalier King Charles Spaniel + Poodle)

A Cavapoo, also known as a Cavoodle, is a hybrid dog breed that results from crossing a Cavalier King Charles Spaniel with a Poodle. The traits of a Cavapoo can vary depending on the parent breeds' characteristics and the specific dog's genetic makeup, but here are some general traits commonly seen in Cavapoos:

Size: Cavapoos are small to medium-sized dogs, typically weighing between 4.5kg to 9kg and standing around 22cm to 35cm tall at the shoulder.

Coat: Cavapoos have a soft, wavy or curly coat that can be hypoallergenic and low-shedding, making them a good choice for people with allergies.

Colour: Cavapoos can come in a variety of colours, including black, white, cream, apricot, and red.

Temperament: Cavapoos are known for their friendly, affectionate, and outgoing personalities. They are good with children and other pets and make excellent family pets.

Exercise needs: Cavapoos have moderate exercise needs and require daily walks and playtime to keep them physically and mentally stimulated.

Health: Like all dog breeds, Cavapoos can be prone to certain health issues, such as hip dysplasia, ear infections, and dental problems. It's essential to buy a Cavapoo puppy from a reputable breeder who tests their breeding dogs for genetic health conditions.

Cavapoos are a popular breed that combines the sweet and gentle nature of the Cavalier King Charles Spaniel with the intelligence and trainability of the Poodle. They make excellent family pets for people who are looking for a small, hypoallergenic dog that is easy to train and loves to play.

Chipoo – (Chihuahua + Poodle)

A Chipoo, also known as a Chihuahua Poodle mix, is a hybrid dog breed that results from crossing a Chihuahua with a Poodle. Here are some general traits commonly seen in Chipoo in metric units:

Size: Chipoo is a small dog breed, typically weighing between 1.5 to 6 kilograms and standing around 15 to 30cm tall at the shoulder.

Coat: Chipoo has a soft, curly or wavy coat that can be long or medium length. They may be hypoallergenic and low-shedding, making them a good choice for people with allergies.

Colour: Chipoo can come in a variety of colours, including black, white, cream, brown, and apricot.

Temperament: Chipoo is known for their affectionate, lively, and loyal personalities. They are good with children and other pets and make excellent family pets.

Exercise needs: Chipoo has moderate exercise needs and require daily walks and playtime to keep them physically and mentally stimulated.

Health: Like all dog breeds, Chipoo can be prone to certain health issues, such as dental problems, patellar luxation, and hypoglycaemia. It's essential to buy a Chipoo puppy from a reputable breeder who tests their breeding dogs for genetic health conditions.

Chipoo is a popular breed that combines the lively and affectionate nature of Chihuahua with the intelligence and trainability of the Poodle. They make excellent family pets for people who are looking for a small, hypoallergenic dog that is easy to train and loves to play.

Doberdoodle– (Doberman Pinscher + Poodle)

It's important to note that dog breeding can result in a wide variety of outcomes, and it's difficult to predict exactly what traits a dog will inherit from each parent. However, here are some general characteristics that might be expected from a Doberman Pinscher-Poodle crossbreed, often referred to as a Doberdoodle:

Size: A Doberdoodle may vary in size depending on the size of the Poodle parent used in the breeding. Standard Poodles are typically used, which can produce a medium to large-sized dog. The weight of a Doberdoodle can range from 20 to 40 kilograms.

Coat: The coat of a Doberdoodle may be curly, wavy, or straight, depending on which parent's coat is dominant. The coat may be hypoallergenic, as Poodles are known for producing low-allergen fur.

Temperament: A Doberdoodle may inherit traits from both parents, resulting in a dog that is energetic, intelligent, and loyal. They *may* also be good with children and make good family pets.

Exercise Needs: A Doberdoodle may require regular exercise to maintain their health and well-being. They may enjoy long walks, runs, or playtime in a large garden.

Grooming: Depending on the type of coat a Doberdoodle inherits, they may require regular grooming to prevent matting or tangling of their fur. Regular brushing and occasional trips to the groomer may be necessary.

It's important to note that individual Doberdoodles can vary in their characteristics, and it's impossible to predict with certainty what traits a specific dog will inherit. It's always best to research both parent breeds and to meet any potential puppies before making a decision to adopt.

Double Doodles (two different doodles)

A Double Doodle is a hybrid dog breed that results from crossbreeding two different Doodle breeds, typically a Goldendoodle and a Labradoodle. Here are some general characteristics of a Double Doodle:

Appearance: Double Doodles can have a variety of coat types, including curly, wavy, and straight, and come in a range of colours. They typically have a medium to large size and a sturdy build.

Temperament: Double Doodles are known for being friendly, sociable, and loyal dogs that get along well with both humans and other pets. They are intelligent and trainable, making them great companions for families or individuals who enjoy spending time outdoors or engaging in activities such as hiking, running, or playing fetch.

Exercise Needs: Double Doodles are a high-energy breed and require regular exercise to stay healthy and happy. They benefit from daily walks, runs, or other forms of physical activity to burn off excess energy.

Grooming Needs: Double Doodles have a curly or wavy coat that requires regular grooming to prevent matting and tangling. They benefit from regular brushing, bathing, and trimming to keep their coat looking healthy and shiny.

Health: Double Doodles are generally considered to be healthy dogs with a lifespan of around 10-15 years. However, as with all breeds, they are prone to certain health issues such as hip dysplasia, eye problems, and skin allergies.

Trainability: Double Doodles are intelligent and eager to please, which makes them easy to train. They respond well to positive reinforcement techniques such as treats and praise and benefit from early socialization and training to develop good behaviours and manners.

Overall, Double Doodles are affectionate, playful, and intelligent dogs that make great family pets and companions for individuals who enjoy an active lifestyle.

Havapoo – (Havanese + Poodle)

The Havanese is a small and sturdy dog breed with a tail carried over its back and ears that drop and fold. The coat is abundant, long, and silky, and comes in all colours. The Havanese is the national dog of Cuba and the country's only native breed. The breed became more widely known when the Communist regime took control of Cuba and many people fled to the USA taking their dogs with them. A Havapoo, also known as a Havanese Poodle mix, is a crossbreed between a Havanese and a Poodle. Like with any crossbreed, traits can vary depending on the specific dog and which traits it inherits from each parent. However, here are some general characteristics of a Havapoo in metric units:

Size: Havapoos are typically small to medium-sized dogs. They can weigh anywhere from 3.5 to 11 kilograms and stand between 20 to 38 centimetres tall.

Coat: The coat of a Havapoo may be curly or wavy, and can be of varying lengths. They may also be hypoallergenic, depending on which parent they inherit their coat from.

Temperament: Havapoos are known to be affectionate, playful, and intelligent dogs. They are often good with children and make great family pets. They may also have a tendency to bark, which can make them good watchdogs.

Exercise Needs: Havapoos require regular exercise to keep them healthy and happy. They may enjoy walks, playtime in the yard, or even playing indoor games.

Grooming: Depending on the length of their coat, Havapoos may require regular grooming to prevent matting or tangling of their fur. They may also require occasional trips to the groomer for haircuts.

It's important to note that individual Havapoos can vary in their characteristics, and it's impossible to predict with certainty what traits a specific dog will inherit. It's always best to research both parent breeds and to meet any potential puppies before making a decision to adopt.

Irish Doodle – (Irish Setter + Poodle)

An Irish Doodle is a crossbreed between an Irish Setter and a Poodle. Like with any crossbreed, traits can vary depending on the specific dog and which traits it inherits from each parent. However, here are some general characteristics of an Irish Doodle in metric units:

Size: Irish Doodles are typically medium to large-sized dogs. They can weigh anywhere from 22 to 32 kilograms and stand between 55 to 65 centimetres tall.

Coat: The coat of an Irish Doodle may be curly or wavy, and can be of varying lengths. They may also be hypoallergenic, depending on which parent they inherit their coat from.

Temperament: Irish Doodles are known to be friendly, loyal, and intelligent dogs. They are often good with children and make great family pets. They may also have a tendency to be protective of their owners.

Exercise Needs: Irish Doodles require regular exercise to keep them healthy and happy. They may enjoy walks, hikes, or playtime in the yard.

Grooming: Depending on the length of their coat, Irish Doodles may require regular grooming to prevent matting or tangling of their fur. They may also require occasional trips to the groomer for haircuts.

Individual Irish Doodles can vary in their characteristics, and it's impossible to predict with certainty what traits a specific dog will inherit. It's always best to research both parent breeds and to meet any potential puppies before making a decision to adopt.

Jack-A-Poo – (Jack Russell Terrier + Poodle)

A Jack-a-poo, also known as a Jack Russell Poodle mix, is a crossbreed between a Jack Russell Terrier and a Poodle. Like with any crossbreed, traits can vary depending on the specific dog and which traits it inherits from each parent. However, here are some general characteristics of a Jack-a-poo in metric units:

Size: Jack-a-poos are typically small to medium-sized dogs. They can weigh anywhere from 3.5 to 9 kilograms and stand between 25 to 38 centimetres tall.

Coat: The coat of a Jack-a-poo may be curly or wavy, and can be of varying lengths. They may also be hypoallergenic, depending on which parent they inherit their coat from.

Temperament: Jack-a-poos are known to be friendly, energetic, and intelligent dogs. They are often good with children and make great family pets. They may also have a tendency to be vocal, which can make them good watchdogs.

Exercise Needs: Jack-a-poos require regular exercise to keep them healthy and happy. They may enjoy walks, playtime in the yard, or even playing indoor games.

Grooming: Depending on the length of their coat, Jack-a-poos may require regular grooming to prevent matting or tangling of their fur. They may also require occasional trips to the groomer for haircuts.

Individual Jack-a-poos can vary in their characteristics, and it's impossible to predict with certainty what traits a specific dog will inherit. It's always best to research both parent breeds and to meet any potential puppies before making a decision to adopt.

Maltipoo – (Maltese + Poodle)

The Maltese is a small and affectionate toy dog breed that hails from the Mediterranean region and is known for its trademark silky, white fur that accentuates its big, dark eyes1 It can make for a charming lapdog, though it does still need daily exercise. The Maltese also can be an alert and fearless watchdog, despite its small size. A Maltipoo is a crossbreed between a Maltese and a Poodle. Like with any crossbreed, traits can vary depending on the specific dog and which traits it inherits from each parent. However, here are some general characteristics of a Maltipoo in metric units:

Size: Maltipoos are typically small dogs. They can weigh anywhere from 2.3 to 4.5 kilograms and stand between 20 to 35 centimetres tall.

Coat: The coat of a Maltipoo is often curly or wavy and can be of varying lengths. They may also be hypoallergenic, depending on which parent they inherit their coat from.

Temperament: Maltipoos are known to be friendly, affectionate, and intelligent dogs. They are often good with children and make great family pets. They may also have a tendency to be vocal, which can make them good watchdogs.

Exercise Needs: Maltipoos require regular exercise to keep them healthy and happy. They may enjoy short walks, playtime in the yard, or even playing indoor games.

Grooming: Maltipoos require regular grooming to prevent matting or tangling of their fur. They may also require occasional trips to the groomer for haircuts.

It's important to note that individual Maltipoos can vary in their characteristics, and it's impossible to predict with certainty what traits a specific dog will inherit. It's always best to research both parent breeds and to meet any potential puppies before making a decision to adopt.

Pekapoo – (Pekingese + Poodle)

The Pekingese is a breed of toy dog, originating in China. The breed was favoured by royalty of the Chinese Imperial court as a companion dog, and its name refers to the city of Peking where the Forbidden City is located. The breed has several characteristics and health issues related to its unique appearance. The Pekapoo, also known as a Pekingese Poodle mix, is a crossbreed between a Pekingese and a Poodle. Like with any crossbreed, traits can vary depending on the specific dog and which traits it inherits from each parent. However, here are some general characteristics of a Pekapoo in metric units:

Size: Pekapoos are typically small dogs. They can weigh anywhere from 3 to 7 kilograms and stand between 20 to 28 centimetres tall.

Coat: The coat of a Pekapoo may be curly or wavy, and can be of varying lengths. They may also be hypoallergenic, depending on which parent they inherit their coat from.

Temperament: Pekapoos are known to be friendly, affectionate, and loyal dogs. They are often good with children and make great family pets. They may also have a tendency to be independent and stubborn at times.

Exercise Needs: Pekapoos require regular exercise to keep them healthy and happy. They may enjoy short walks, playtime in the yard, or even playing indoor games.

Grooming: Pekapoos require regular grooming to prevent matting or tangling of their fur. They may also require occasional trips to the groomer for haircuts.

Individual Pekapoos can vary in their characteristics, and it's impossible to predict with certainty what traits a specific dog will inherit. It's always best to research both parent breeds and to meet any potential puppies before making a decision to adopt.

Pomapoo – (Pomeranian + Poodle)

A Pomapoo is a crossbreed between a Pomeranian and a Poodle. The Pomeranian (often known as a Pom) is a breed of dog of the Spitz type that is named for the Pomerania region in north-west Poland and north-east Germany in Central Europe. Classed as a toy dog breed because of its small size, the Pomeranian is descended from larger Spitz-type dogs. Pomeranians are small dogs that boast a thick plush coat. They are easily recognized by their luxuriant fluffy double coat and foxy face with alert, prick ears. They are true "toy" dogs, with an ideal height of 20-25cm and weight of only 1 to 3kg.

Like with any crossbreed, traits can vary depending on the specific dog and which traits it inherits from each parent. However, here are some general characteristics of a Pomapoo in metric units:

Size: Pomapoos are typically small dogs. They can weigh anywhere from 2 to 5 kilograms and stand between 20 to 25 centimetres tall.

Coat: The coat of a Pomapoo may be curly or wavy, and can be of varying lengths. They may also be hypoallergenic, depending on which parent they inherit their coat from.

Temperament: Pomapoos are known to be affectionate, playful, and intelligent dogs. They are often good with children and make great family pets. They may also have a tendency to be vocal, which can make them good watchdogs.

Exercise Needs: Pomapoos require regular exercise to keep them healthy and happy. They may enjoy short walks, playtime in the yard, or even playing indoor games.

Grooming: Pomapoos require regular grooming to prevent matting or tangling of their fur. They may also require occasional trips to the groomer for haircuts.

Individual Pomapoos can vary in their characteristics, and it's impossible to predict with certainty what traits a specific dog will inherit. It's always best to research both parent breeds and to meet any potential puppies before making a decision to adopt.

Scoodle – (Scottish Terrier + Poodle)

A Scoodle, also known as a Scottish Terrier Poodle mix, is a crossbreed between a Scottish Terrier and a Poodle. Like with any crossbreed, traits can vary depending on the specific dog and which traits it inherits from each parent. However, here are some general characteristics of a Scoodle in metric units:

Size: Scoodles are typically small to medium-sized dogs. They can weigh anywhere from 4 to 10 kilograms and stand between 25 to 40 centimetres tall.

Coat: The coat of a Scoodle may be curly or wavy, and can be of varying lengths. They may also be hypoallergenic, depending on which parent they inherit their coat from.

Temperament: Scoodles are known to be friendly, affectionate, and intelligent dogs. They are often good with children and make great family pets. They may also have a tendency to be independent and stubborn at times.

Exercise Needs: Scoodles require regular exercise to keep them healthy and happy. They may enjoy short walks, playtime in the yard, or even playing indoor games.

Grooming: Scoodles require regular grooming to prevent matting or tangling of their fur. They may also require occasional trips to the groomer for haircuts.

Individual Scoodles can vary in their characteristics, and it's impossible to predict with certainty what traits a specific dog will inherit. It's always best to research both parent breeds and to meet any potential puppies before making a decision to adopt.

Shih-poo – (Shih Tzu + Poodle)

The Shih Tzu is a toy dog breed originating from Tibet and was bred from the Pekingese and the Lhasa Apso. They are known for their short snouts and large round eyes, as well as their long coat, floppy ears, and short and stout posture. The breed is also known for its friendly and outgoing personality.

The Shih Tzu is a brachycephalic breed (that is, it has a very short muzzle), which makes it susceptible to brachycephalic airway obstruction syndrome which may be caused by abnormally small nostril openings, a narrow windpipe, and an excessively long soft palate in relation to the head.

A Shihpoo, also known as a Shih Tzu Poodle mix, is a crossbreed between a Shih Tzu and a Poodle. Like with any crossbreed, traits can vary depending on the specific dog and which traits it inherits from each parent.

Size: Shihpoos are typically small dogs. They can weigh anywhere from 3 to 7 kilograms and stand between 20 to 28 centimetres tall.

Coat: The coat of a Shihpoo may be curly or wavy, and can be of varying lengths. They may also be hypoallergenic, depending on which parent they inherit their coat from.

Temperament: Shihpoos are known to be friendly, affectionate, and intelligent dogs. They are often good with children and make great family pets. They may also have a tendency to be vocal, which can make them good watchdogs.

Exercise Needs: Shihpoos require regular exercise to keep them healthy and happy. They may enjoy short walks, playtime in the yard, or even playing indoor games.

Grooming: Shihpoos require regular grooming to prevent matting or tangling of their fur. They may also require occasional trips to the groomer for haircuts.

Individual Shihpoos can vary in their characteristics, and it's impossible to predict with certainty what traits a specific dog will inherit. It's always best to research both parent breeds and to meet any potential puppies before making a decision to adopt.

How and where to buy a dog

There are several methods and places where you can buy a dog. Each method and place has its pros and cons, and it's important to consider these before making a decision.

Breeders: Breeders are individuals or businesses that specialise in breeding and selling dogs. They can offer a wide variety of breeds and can provide information on the dog's lineage, health history, and temperament. However, it's important to do research and find a reputable breeder who prioritizes the welfare of their dogs. See the section on finding a dog breeder below.

Pros: Wide variety of breeds, access to information about the dog's history, health, and temperament.

Cons: May be expensive, may support overbreeding if not reputable, may be far away or require shipping.

Rescue Shelters: Rescue shelters are organizations that take in dogs that have been abandoned, surrendered, or rescued from abusive situations. Adopting a dog from a rescue shelter can be a rewarding experience, as you are giving a second chance to a dog in need. However, shelter dogs may have behavioural issues or health problems, and it may take time and patience to help them adjust to their new home.

Pros: Saving a life, often less expensive, may already be trained, may be microchipped and vaccinated.

Cons: May have health or behavioural problems, may not know the dog's history or breed, may be more difficult to find a specific breed.

Pet Stores: Pet stores are no longer a common place to buy dogs, however they may still be an option depending on where you live. They typically offer a variety of breeds and sizes, and you can often see and interact with the puppies before making a purchase. However, pet stores are often criticised for supporting puppy mills, which are large-scale breeding operations that prioritize profit over the welfare of the dogs. Dogs from puppy mills are often kept in poor conditions and may have health and behaviour problems.

Pros: Easy to find, many options, chance to interact with puppies before buying.

Cons: Supports puppy mills, may have unhealthy dogs, may have behavioural problems.

Online Marketplaces: There are many online marketplaces where you can buy dogs, such as Craigslist or Facebook Marketplace. While these platforms can offer a wide variety of breeds and may be convenient, it's important to be cautious and do research to avoid scams or buying from puppy mills.

Pros: Many options, can be convenient, may find a good deal.

Cons: May support puppy mills, may not know the dog's history or health, may be scams or fraudulent listings.

how to find a good dog breeder

Finding a good dog breeder can be a daunting task, but here are some steps you can take to help ensure that you find a responsible and reputable breeder:

Research the breed you are interested in: Before you start looking for a breeder, it's important to research the breed you are interested in. This will help you to understand the breed's temperament, exercise needs, health issues and other important factors that will help you determine if the breed is right for you.

Check breed club websites: Most breed clubs have websites that provide information on responsible breeders. These breeders will typically follow the club's code of ethics, which includes breeding for health and temperament, and providing proper care for their dogs.

Ask for referrals: Ask friends, family members or acquaintances who have dogs if they can recommend a good breeder. If you see a dog you like, ask the owner where they got their dog from.

Attend dog shows: Attend dog shows or events to meet breeders and see their dogs in person. This will give you a chance to talk to breeders and see how they interact with their dogs.

Ask questions: Once you have found a breeder, ask them lots of questions. Ask about their breeding program, health testing, and what kind of socialisation and training they provide for their puppies.

Visit the breeder: If possible, visit the breeder in person to see their facilities and meet their dogs. This will give you a chance to see if the breeder is responsible and caring, and to get a sense of the conditions in which the dogs are raised.

Check references: Ask the breeder for references from previous puppy buyers. Contact these people to ask about their experience with the breeder and their puppies.

Remember, a good breeder will always put the health and welfare of their dogs first and will be happy to answer your questions and provide you with information about their breeding program.

The costs of dog ownership

The costs of dog ownership can vary depending on factors such as the breed, size, age, and health of the dog, as well as the owner's lifestyle and location. Here are some of the main costs associated with owning a dog and the typical annual costs of dog ownership in the UK:

Purchase or adoption fees: If you're purchasing a purebred dog from a breeder, the cost can range from a few hundred to several thousand pounds depending on the breed. Adopting a dog from a shelter or rescue organization is usually less expensive, but there may still be an adoption fee.

Food: Depending on the size and breed of your dog, the cost of food can range from around £200 to £1,000 per year.

Vet bills: Annual veterinary expenses can range from £200 to £1,000 or more, depending on the dog's health and any necessary treatments or procedures.

The cost of vet bills for a puppy in its first year will depend on several factors such as the breed, size, and health of the puppy. However, here are some typical vet bills that a puppy owner can expect in their first year:

Initial vaccinations: Puppies need a series of vaccinations to protect against diseases like distemper, parvovirus, and rabies. The cost of initial vaccinations can range from £50 to £100.

Booster vaccinations: Puppies require booster vaccinations to maintain immunity to certain diseases. The cost of booster vaccinations can range from £50 to £100.

Spaying or neutering: The cost of spaying or neutering a puppy can range from £100 to £300, depending on the size and gender of the puppy.

Microchipping: Microchipping is a legal requirement in the UK, and the cost can range from £20 to £50.

Health checks: Puppies require regular health checks to ensure that they are growing and developing properly. The cost of health checks can range from £30 to £50 per visit.

Worming and flea treatments: Puppies require regular worming and flea treatments to prevent infestations. The cost of these treatments can range from £20 to £50 per treatment.

Overall, the cost of vet bills for a puppy in its first year can range from around £300 to £800, depending on the puppy's individual needs. It's important to budget for these costs before getting a puppy, and to ensure that you are able to provide for their ongoing healthcare needs throughout their life.

Pet insurance: Pet insurance can cost between £100 to £300 per year, depending on the level of coverage.

Grooming: The cost of grooming will depend on the breed of dog and how often they need to be groomed. For example, regular grooming for a long-haired breed can cost around £300 per year.

Supplies: This includes things like collars, leashes, toys, and bedding, and can cost around £100 to £200 per year.

Training and behaviour: The cost of training and behaviour classes can range from around £100 to £500 or more, depending on the type and length of classes.

Boarding and pet sitting: If you need to board your dog or use a pet-sitting service, this can cost anywhere from £10 to £50 per day.

Overall, the cost of owning a dog in the UK can range from around £1,000 to £2,000 per year, or more if the dog requires extensive medical treatment or has special needs.

Equipment needed

As a dog owner, you'll need a variety of equipment and supplies to keep your furry friend healthy and happy. Here are some of the essential items you'll need:

Collar and lead: Every dog needs a collar and lead for walking and identification purposes. Collars should be properly fitted and have identification tags with your contact information.

Harness: A harness can be a good alternative to a collar and leash for dogs that tend to pull or have respiratory issues. Choose a harness that's well-fitted and comfortable for your dog.

Crate: A crate can provide a safe and comfortable space for your dog to relax or sleep in. Choose a crate that's the appropriate size for your dog and provides plenty of ventilation and room to move around.

Bedding: Your dog will need a comfortable place to sleep and relax. A dog bed or blanket can provide a cosy spot for your furry friend.

Food and water bowls: Choose food and water bowls that are the appropriate size for your dog and are easy to clean. Stainless steel or ceramic bowls are a good choice.

Grooming supplies: Depending on your dog's breed, you may need grooming supplies like brushes, combs, shampoo, and nail clippers.

Toys: Dogs need mental and physical stimulation, and toys can provide both. Choose toys that are appropriate for your dog's size and age.

Overall, the cost of dog ownership can range from a few hundred to several thousand pounds per year depending on your dog's needs and your lifestyle. It's important to consider these costs before bringing a dog into your home and to budget accordingly to ensure that you can provide the best care for your furry friend.

Types of Dog Harness

There are several types of dog harnesses available, each designed to suit different purposes and dog breeds. Here are some of the most common types of dog harnesses:

Back-clip harness: This type of harness features a D-ring on the back and is typically used for walking dogs that are already trained not to pull. Back-clip harnesses are comfortable for most dogs and can be easy to put on and take off.

Front-clip harness: This type of harness features a D-ring on the front and is often used for dogs that pull on the leash. Front-clip harnesses can help to reduce pulling and provide more control over your dog's movement.

Dual-clip harness: A dual-clip harness features both a front and back D-ring, providing the flexibility to use either one. This type of harness is great for training and can be used to provide more control over your dog's movement.

No-pull harness: This type of harness is designed specifically to reduce pulling on the leash. No-pull harnesses typically feature a front D-ring and/or a tightening mechanism that discourages pulling.

Step-in harness: A step-in harness is designed to be put on by having your dog step into it and then securing it around the chest and back. This type of harness is easy to put on and can be a good choice for dogs that don't like things going over their head.

Vest harness: A vest harness is designed to be worn like a vest and typically features a back D-ring. Vest harnesses can be comfortable for dogs and provide a snug fit.

Overall, choosing the right type of harness for your dog will depend on their breed, size, and behaviour.

Where will the dog sleep?

It is generally not recommended for a puppy to sleep in the owner's bed. While some people may enjoy having their puppy snuggle up with them at night, there are several potential problems with this:

Reinforcing bad behaviour: Allowing your puppy to sleep in your bed can reinforce bad habits, such as jumping up on the bed without permission, begging for attention or food, and barking or whining for attention.

Disrupting sleep: Puppies are often restless and may wake up frequently during the night, which can disrupt the owner's sleep and lead to fatigue and irritability.

Health risks: Puppies may carry harmful bacteria or parasites that can be transmitted to humans, particularly if the puppy is not fully vaccinated or dewormed.

Separation anxiety: Allowing your puppy to sleep in your bed can create a dependence on the owner's presence and make it harder for the puppy to adjust to being alone or sleeping in a separate area.

Instead of allowing the puppy to sleep in the owner's bed, it is recommended to provide the puppy with a designated sleeping area, such as a crate or a dog bed in a quiet, comfortable part of the house. This will help the puppy develop good habits and give them a sense of security and comfort. Over time, the puppy can gradually be trained to sleep on their own, with the owner nearby, until they are comfortable sleeping alone.

Both a dog bed and a crate can be beneficial for a dog, but it depends on the individual dog's needs and preferences. Here are some factors to consider when deciding whether a dog should have a bed or a crate or both:

Comfort: Dogs need a comfortable place to rest, and a bed can provide a soft and cosy spot for them to sleep. A crate can also provide a comfortable and secure place for a dog to rest.

Safety: A crate can be useful for keeping a dog safe when you are not able to supervise them, such as when you are away from home or at night. A crate can also be helpful for managing destructive or anxious behaviour.

Training: Crate training can be a useful tool for house training a puppy or teaching a dog to settle down and relax. A bed can also be used as a reward for good behaviour and as a place for a dog to retreat when they need some alone time.

Space: If you have limited space in your home, a crate can be a good way to provide a designated sleeping area for your dog while also keeping them contained and out of the way.

it's a good idea to provide your dog with both a bed and a crate, so they have the option of choosing where to rest depending on their mood and needs. You can also use a crate and a bed together, with the bed inside the crate, to create a cosy and secure sleeping area for your dog. However, every dog is different, so it's important to observe your dog's behaviour and preferences to determine what works best for them.

Training your dog

There are several options for dog training, each with its own benefits. Here are some of the most common options:

Puppy classes: Puppy classes are typically held for dogs between 8 and 16 weeks old and focus on socialization and basic obedience training. These classes are a great way to introduce your puppy to other dogs and people, and to teach them basic commands like sit, stay, and come.

Benefits: Puppy classes help your puppy develop important socialization skills and learn basic commands, which can make future training easier.

Group obedience classes: Group obedience classes are typically held for dogs over 16 weeks old and focus on basic obedience training. These classes are usually taught in a group setting and cover commands like sit, stay, come, and heel.

Benefits: Group obedience classes are a great way to socialize your dog and help them learn basic obedience skills. They can also be a fun way to bond with your dog and meet other dog owners.

Private training: Private training sessions are typically one-on-one sessions with a professional dog trainer. These sessions can be customized to your dog's individual needs and can cover a range of training topics.

Benefits: Private training sessions are a great way to address specific training issues and get individualised attention for your dog. They can also be more convenient for busy owners who may not be able to attend group classes.

Board and train: Board and train programs involve sending your dog to a professional trainer for an extended period of time, typically 2-4 weeks. During this time, the trainer will work with your dog on obedience training and behaviour modification.

Benefits: Board and train programs can be a good option for busy owners who don't have time to devote to training, or for dogs with serious behaviour issues that require intensive training.

Online training: Online training programs involve accessing training materials and resources through the internet. These programs may include video tutorials, virtual training sessions, and other resources.

Benefits: Online training programs can be a convenient option for owners who may not have access to in-person training or who prefer to train their dog at their own pace.

Mental Stimulation

No matter which option you choose, dog training can have many benefits, including improved behaviour, better communication between you and your dog, and a stronger bond with your furry friend. Well-trained dogs are also more confident and well-behaved, which can make them better companions and easier to manage in a variety of settings.

All dogs require some level of mental stimulation to keep them happy and healthy, but some breeds are known to need more mental stimulation than others. Here are some dog breeds that typically require more mental stimulation:

Border Collie: Border Collies are a herding breed that are known for their high intelligence and energy levels. They require a lot of mental stimulation and activities that challenge their minds, such as training exercises, puzzle toys, and games of fetch.

Australian Shepherd: Australian Shepherds are another herding breed that are highly intelligent and active. They need mental stimulation to prevent boredom and destructive behaviours, and activities such as obedience training, agility courses, and interactive toys can help keep them mentally engaged.

Poodle: Poodles are a versatile breed that come in a variety of sizes, and are known for their intelligence and trainability. They require mental stimulation to prevent boredom, and activities such as obedience training, trick training, and puzzle toys can help keep them engaged.

Jack Russell Terrier: Jack Russell Terriers are a small breed that are known for their high energy levels and intelligence. They require mental stimulation to prevent boredom and destructive behaviours, and activities such as agility training, obedience training, and interactive toys can help keep them engaged.

Shetland Sheepdog: Shetland Sheepdogs are a herding breed that are known for their intelligence and affectionate nature. They require mental stimulation to prevent boredom, and activities such as obedience training, agility courses, and interactive toys can help keep them mentally engaged.

Of course, every dog is an individual and their needs for mental stimulation may vary based on factors such as their age, personality, and lifestyle. It's important to provide your dog with enough mental and physical exercise to keep them happy and healthy.

How will a dog affect my lifestyle

Adopting a dog will definitely affect your lifestyle, as you will need to make some adjustments to accommodate your new furry friend. Here are some ways that a dog might affect your lifestyle:

Daily routine: Having a dog means that you will need to adjust your daily routine to include time for feeding, walking, and playing with your dog. You will need to consider your dog's needs when planning your day and be prepared to dedicate time to caring for them.

Exercise: Dogs require regular exercise to stay healthy, which means that you will need to incorporate daily walks or trips to the park into your routine. This can be a great way to get more exercise yourself, as you will likely be walking or running with your dog.

Social life: Depending on your lifestyle, having a dog might affect your social life. You will need to consider your dog's needs when planning social events or outings, and may need to arrange for someone to care for your dog while you're away.

Travel: If you enjoy traveling, having a dog might require more planning and preparation. You will need to make arrangements for your dog's care while you're away, or bring them along on your travels if possible.

Expenses: Caring for a dog can be expensive, with costs including food, veterinary care, grooming, and supplies. You will need to budget for these expenses and be prepared to provide your dog with the care they need.

Owning a dog also comes with many benefits, including companionship, improved mental and physical health, and a sense of purpose and responsibility. If you are willing to make the necessary adjustments to your lifestyle, owning a dog can be a rewarding experience that enhances your life in many ways.

Feeding a dog

When it comes to feeding your dog, there are several options to consider, each with its own benefits and drawbacks. Here's a rundown of the most common feeding options for dogs:

Dry food: Dry food, also known as kibble, is the most common type of dog food. It's convenient, easy to store, and can be left out for your dog to graze on throughout the day. Most commercial dry dog foods are nutritionally balanced and provide a complete diet for your dog. However, some dogs may find it difficult to digest, and it may not be as tasty as wet food.

Wet food: Wet food, also known as canned food, is another popular option for feeding dogs. It's often more flavourful than dry food and can be easier to digest for dogs with sensitive stomachs. However, it can be more expensive than dry food, and may spoil more quickly once opened.

Raw food: Some dog owners choose to feed their dogs a raw food diet, which consists of raw meats, bones, fruits, and vegetables. Proponents of raw food diets argue that it's a more natural diet for dogs and can improve their overall health. However, raw food diets can be time-consuming to prepare, and there are risks associated with handling raw meat.

Homemade food: Some dog owners choose to make their own dog food at home, using recipes that include cooked meats, vegetables, and grains. Homemade food can be a good option for dogs with specific dietary needs or allergies, and it allows you to control the ingredients that go into your dog's food. However, homemade food can be time-consuming to prepare, and it's important to ensure that it provides a balanced diet for your dog.

Combination diet: Many dog owners choose to combine different types of food to provide their dogs with a varied diet. For example, you might feed your dog a mix of dry food and wet food, or add some fresh fruits and vegetables to their kibble. A combination diet can provide the benefits of different types of food, but it's important to ensure that your dog is still getting a balanced diet overall.

Jokes

This wouldn't be a Paul Hill book if it didn't have a joke in it....

Once my dog ate all the Scrabble tiles.
For days he kept leaving little messages around the house.

What's the difference between a businessman and a hot dog?
The businessman wears a suit but the dog just pants.

Why didn't the dog want to play football?
It was a Boxer.

Which dog breed is Dracula's favourite?
Bloodhound.

Why did the two-legged dog come to an abrupt halt?
It had two paws.

I asked my dog what's two minus two?
He said nothing

What do you get when you cross a Cocker Spaniel, a Poodle, and a Rooster?
A Cockerpoodledoo!

Why was the cat afraid of the tree?
Because of it's bark.

Why did the dog sit in the shade?
He didn't want to be a hot dog!

Why did the dog wear a bell around his neck?
He was a little husky!

What do you call a dog who loves bubble baths?
A Shampoodle!

Why did the dog join the circus?
He wanted to be a paw-former!

What did the dog say when he sat on sandpaper?
"Ruff!"

What kind of dog can tell time?
A watchdog!

Why do dogs make terrible dancers?
Because they have two left feet... and two right feet!

Afterword

A faithful friend that's always near,
A furry companion that brings you cheer,
A four-legged buddy with a wagging tail,
A loyal companion that never fails.

The benefits of dog ownership are many,
From the joy they bring to the love they give plenty,
They're always there to comfort and support,
Through thick and thin, they'll never fall short.

Dogs teach us lessons about loyalty and love,
About how to live in the moment, to just be and love,
They show us the simple pleasures of life,
And help us through the struggles and strife.

They bring us laughter, happiness, and fun,
And remind us of the beauty of a life well done,
With them by our side, we feel strong and brave,
A bond that's unbreakable, a love that will never fade.

So if you're looking for a companion true,
A friend that will always be there for you,
Consider a dog, for they're more than just pets,
They're family, love, and happiness, you won't regret.

The End

Please watch out for my next book